BROWN RATS,
BLACK RATS

BROWN RATS, BLACK RATS

by Jane Annixter and Paul Annixter

illustrated by Gilbert Riswold

Prentice-Hall, Inc.,
Englewood Cliffs, New Jersey

Printed in the United States of America
Prentice-Hall International, Inc., London
Prentice-Hall of Australia, Pty. Ltd., North Sydney
Prentice-Hall of Canada, Ltd., Toronto
Prentice-Hall of India Private Ltd., New Delhi
Prentice-Hall of Japan, Inc., Tokyo
Prentice-Hall of Southeast Asia Pte. Ltd., Singapore
10 9 8 7 6 5 4 3 2 1
Library of Congress Cataloging in Publication Data

Annixter, Jane.
    Brown rats, black rats.

    SUMMARY: Text and illustrations trace the
natural and social history of the dreaded
companions of mankind, the brown and black rats.
    1. Rattus norvegicus—Juvenile literature.
2. Rattus rattus—Juvenile literature. [1. Rats]
I. Annixter, Paul, joint author. II. Riswold,
Gilbert. III. Title.
QL737.R666A56   599′.3233   77-4412
ISBN 0-13-084400-4

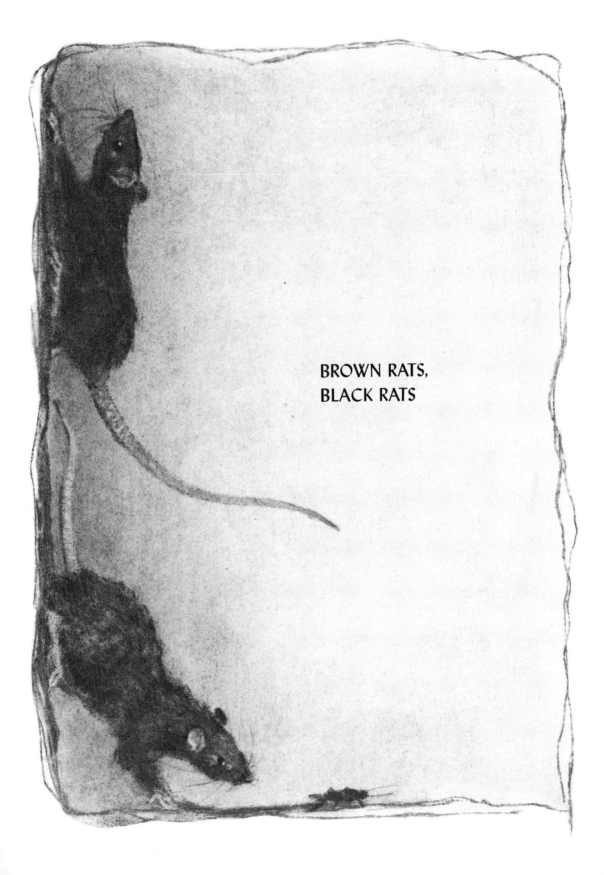

BROWN RATS,
BLACK RATS

Rats Chew To
Keep Their Teeth Short

Rats gnaw walls, lead pipes, furniture, floors, plaster, roofs, foundations, the insulation on electric cables, books, paintings, clothes, and rugs. Their ceaseless gnawing

causes flooding and fires and has even been known to cause the collapse of buildings. Rats *have* to gnaw all the time. As with other rodents, their front teeth never stop growing. Since its teeth grow five inches every year, a rat has to grind them down or it would soon be unable to close its mouth.

Rats Attack Other Animals

In a henhouse rats will slaughter dozens of chicks and hens and then leave the dead birds strewn about. They bite defenseless farm animals. Rats will attack almost any animal that cannot defend itself, even

an elephant. Many elephants have died of infection caused by rat-bite to their trunks. Rats seem to know when there is a sick, helpless person in a house. They have been known to watch through a hole till that person is alone and unprotected, then attack and gnaw them to death. Babies and young children have been eaten alive by rats, and each year some fourteen thousand people are bitten by them. Some of those bites are fatal.

Rats are said to prefer soft foods, but they will eat anything. If human beings fed themselves in proportion to what rats eat, the world's food supply would soon be exhausted. Rats eat a third of their weight every day. Not only do they eat millions of tons of good food, they pollute many times that much. Out in the country, whole crops of grain and feed are ruined by rat droppings. In cities, sewer rats gnaw their way into storage rooms and kitchens—nibbling, spilling, scattering wherever they go. In cupboards dry food packages are torn open and spilled. Rats do the same with bins of flour, barrels of sugar and bags of rice—eat a little, spoil a lot. They will take one bite from each apple or potato until a whole winter's food supply is fit only for the public dump where other rats will find it.

City Rats

There are nearly 300 species of rats, most of which live in the wild. Two kinds are familiar to city people, the Brown rat which burrows into cellars and lives in sewers, and the Black, sometimes called the roof or ship

rat, which prefers high places like attics and rooftops. The Black rat has a hairless tail longer than its body, big ears, a sharp snout and soft black or dark-gray fur. Both Black and Brown rats have very sharp hearing, both can swim and climb, and both live near people. If there is plenty to eat, a rat will keep to a small area of no more than 150 feet in diameter. But if food runs short, it will move to the nearest human dwelling and gnaw its way into the house.

Rats Lived With
Cave Men Too

Rats are among the oldest creatures on the evolutionary chain. Small bones have been discovered in caves with ancient human bones, indicating that rats lived with primitive man. Whether they were a curse to the caveman is not known, but terrible things happened when Black rats invaded Europe a few centuries ago.

Both Black and Brown rats came from Asia. In a year of drought when food was scarce a colony of Black rats stowed away in a sailing ship bound for European ports. Other rats followed. They could swim, they could climb ropes and they could eat anything. The rats thrived on ships. From wharves and ports, the rats spread across Europe on the ships that had become their homes.

Terrible Times

At first people regarded the rodents as a harmless nuisance—until their children were bitten and food stores ruined. In those early times it was not known that the fleas and lice carried by rats and transmitted to humans, brought fatal disease. Those who ate the rat-contaminated food became desperately ill and many died. There were epidemics of typhus and Bubonic plague—called the Black Death.

When it was finally realized that rats carried the plague, people fought the pests in every way they knew. Poisons were concocted, traps were set. Rat catchers became so numerous that they had to be organized into guilds. The best Rat Catchers became important city officials. Bounty was offered. An annual tribute in the form of five thousand rat-tails brought special privileges and rewards. But more and more rats came. In London alone an epidemic killed a hundred thousand people. Europe lost a quarter of its entire population.

One early scientist sensed a relationship between disease and the filth in which people lived. He warned his community to burn all their garbage and to keep their city clean. When this was done, the rats of that community promptly moved to a neighboring town. In the clean village the Black Death rate lowered to 5 percent, but elsewhere human waste and filth encouraged the rats to remain. In five or six generations the plague killed thirty-four million people.

What finally drove the Black rat out of the country was the arrival of the Brown rat, also called the Norway rat. The Brown rat was larger, fiercer and more destructive than the Black rat it drove out of Europe.

Rats In America

Rats came to America with the early settlers. They traveled in the holds of ships. When human moves were made to new territory the rats went along too, and started colonies of their own wherever the people settled—on farms, in cities and towns. Rats crossed the Continent with the pioneers. Rats traveled in the first trains. They swam across rivers and lakes to still newer settlements, eating everything that the people ate, the food of other animals and

fields of standing grain. They always lived as close as possible to human beings and always, always increased their numbers.

When cities installed sewage systems on a large scale, Brown rats moved right into the sewers. Black rats used cables as a convenient way of getting from place to place.

We have vaccines now to protect people, but the diseases rats carry still infect us. Rabies, jaundice and rat bite fever are a few of the diseases the gnawing rat brings.

Rats Are Smart

Self-preservation is instinctive but a thorough job of it takes brains as well. Sailors have always declared that rats know when a ship is in bad condition and will abandon it if necessary. The same is true of a condemned building. When the non-climbing mongoose was introduced into

Hawaii to deal with the rat problem, the Brown rats learned how to climb! Another sign of rat intelligence: if a rat is handed a piece of bread too long to fit between the bars of its cage, it will take it, turn it lengthwise, and slip it through the bars.

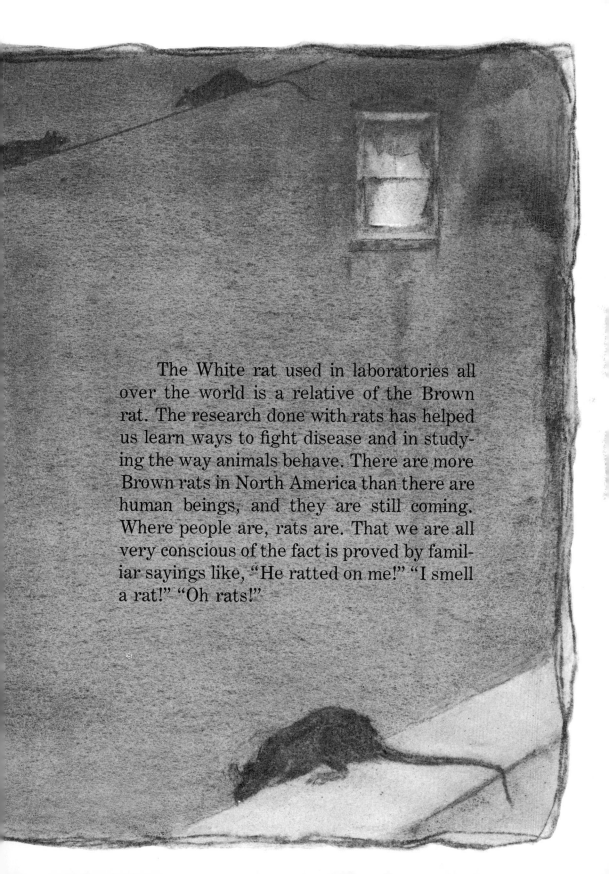

The White rat used in laboratories all over the world is a relative of the Brown rat. The research done with rats has helped us learn ways to fight disease and in studying the way animals behave. There are more Brown rats in North America than there are human beings, and they are still coming. Where people are, rats are. That we are all very conscious of the fact is proved by familiar sayings like, "He ratted on me!" "I smell a rat!" "Oh rats!"

Spooky Rat Noises

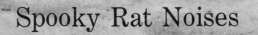

Rats in hollow walls have convinced many people that ghosts walk at night. Houses have been sold by scared owners who did not admit what was driving them away. Even when it is known what the squeaks and scufflings are, the sounds rats make can be pretty scarey. One night rats robbed a small grocer of sixty pounds of walnuts and then stored them in his own walls. For days the grocer was unnerved by noises like rattling bones and clicking teeth—made by his stolen walnuts being rolled around and cracked.

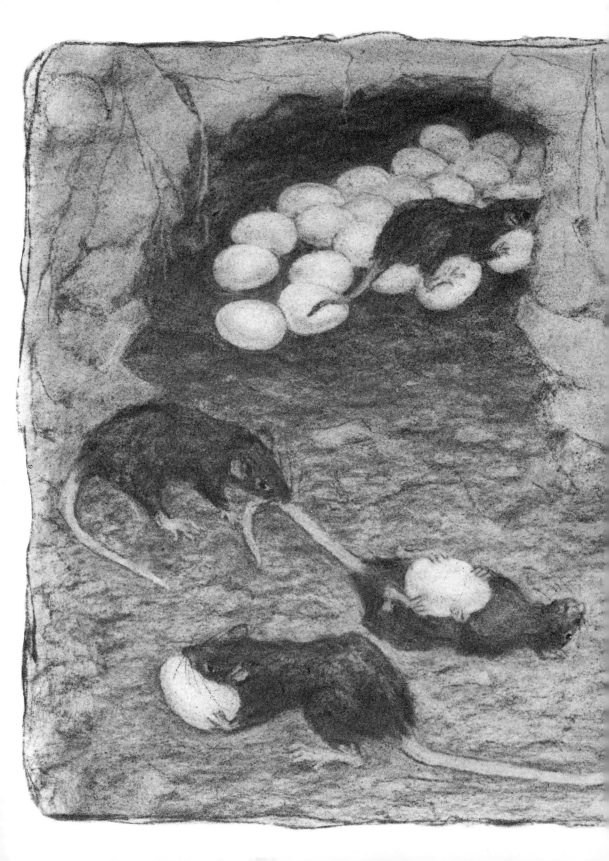

Rats Look Out
For Themselves

Colonies of rats have leaders, usually the strongest rat. Although weak or sick rats are generally left alone, "criminal" or "stupid" rats whose behavior might threaten the survival of the group are killed off. Working together, rats solve difficult problems. Two rats steal eggs. Eggs are hard to transport without breakage, but rats have a system: one rats holds the egg in his forepaws and rolls over, another rat drags him by the tail, egg and all, to their hole. A hatchery is said to have lost almost one thousand eggs over a period of time and then found them again, stock-piled, in rat warrens underground.

Rat Power

Imagine a pair of common Brown rats ten inches long, not counting their hairless tails, each weighing slightly more than a pound. They have coarse brown-gray fur, small ears and rounded snouts. The male is larger, the female is fatter. This pair gnaws a hole in a wall, or digs into a trash heap to make a nest. In just three weeks after the nest is built, mother rat will give birth to ten rat babies. In less than five months these rat babies will be producing litters of their own. Although rats usually live for only one year, in that time the original Brown rat pair will have around 15,000 descendents! The rat's incredible power to reproduce has made the species humanity's number one enemy. As much as we would like to look the other way, we should learn as much about rats as we can.

Are Rats Here To Stay?

Some rats, which scientists call "super rats", have even developed resistance to poison. They can be given 100 times the amount of poison it would take to kill a normal rat and still survive.

Normal rats have an amazing ability to detect harmful or poisoned food. If a rat suspects that even the tiniest morsel of his dinner might be harmful he will starve rather than eat it.

New methods of extermination continue to be invented, but the "war on rats" which human beings have waged for so many centuries is never won.